SUCCESS SECRETS
OF THE
GREAT MASTERS

SUCCESS SECRETS
OF THE
GREAT MASTERS

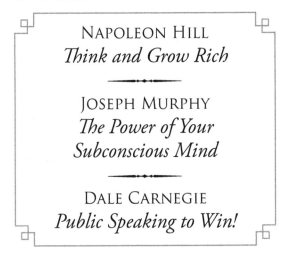

NAPOLEON HILL
Think and Grow Rich

JOSEPH MURPHY
*The Power of Your
Subconscious Mind*

DALE CARNEGIE
Public Speaking to Win!

ABRIDGED AND INTRODUCED BY
MITCH HOROWITZ

MEDIA

Published by Gildan Media LLC
aka G&D Media.
www.GandDmedia.com

Think and Grow Rich was originally published in 1937
The Power of Your Subconscious Mind was originally published in 1963
Public Speaking to Win! was originally published in 1926 as
Public Speaking: A Practical Course for Business Men
G&D Media Condensed Classics editions published 2019
Abridgement and Introduction copyright © 2019 by Mitch Horowitz

FIRST EDITION: 2019

Cover design by David Rheinhardt of Pyrographx

Interior design by Meghan Day Healey of Story Horse, LLC.

ISBN: 978-1-7225-0187-7

Contents

Introduction

A Life Change Awaits You
By Mitch Horowitz

Can a book change a life? From experience, I know that it can. The three books condensed into this collection—*Think and Grow Rich; The Power of Your Subconscious Mind; and Public Speaking to Win!*—have exercised tremendous influence over me as a writer, artist, and businessperson. Collectively, they have dramatically improved my life. In these abridgments, each done with veneration for the author's vision, I have retained exactly what I learned.

I want to share with you my discoveries—and I think when you are done with *Success Secrets of the Great Masters*, you will be prepared to add your own.

- I once reduced Napoleon Hill's *Think and Grow Rich* to a single sentence: "Emotionalized thought directed toward one passionately held aim—aided by organized planning and the Master Mind—is the root of all accomplishment." I ask you to hold that in mind and return to it as you experience this condensation of Hill's classic program. No one has done more than Hill to arrange the mental principles of success into one core curriculum.

- Joseph Murphy's *The Power of Your Subconscious Mind* is the perfect mystical adjunct to Hill. In a manner that is infectious and persuasive, Murphy contends that your subconscious mind is an engine of causation, and that once you impress the subconscious with an aim or wish it devises methods of progress and unfoldment that, at times, seem astounding. This is a principle with which Hill agreed.

- Finally, this collection contains an abridgment of Dale Carnegie's original public-speaking course, here titled *Public Speaking to Win!* Carnegie's lessons taught me the overarching power of *preparation* not only in devising a public talk but in every undertaking in life. The genius of Carnegie's lesson plan is that—like all great ethical and performance-based lessons—it transcends the concerns of its title to become an overall guide to personal effectiveness in every facet of life: work, relationships, and creativity.

If you study these abridgments carefully you will enter into the most powerful inspirational and motivational lessons to emerge from the self-help field. Will they change your life? Begin and find out.

Mitch Horowitz is a PEN Award-winning historian and the author of books including *The Miracle Club: How Thoughts Become Reality.* He edits and introduces G&D Media's line of Condensed Classics and is the author of the Napoleon Hill Success Course series, including *The Miracle of a Definite Chief Aim* and *The Power of the Master Mind.*

THINK
AND
GROW RICH

THINK
AND
GROW RICH

by Napoleon Hill

The Original 1937 Classic
Abridged and Introduced
by Mitch Horowitz

THE CONDENSED CLASSICS LIBRARY™

Contents

The Power of a Single Book

The book you are about to experience has probably touched more lives than any other work of modern self-help. Try a small personal experiment: Carry a copy of *Think and Grow Rich* with you through an airport, grocery store, shopping mall, or any public place—and see if more than one person doesn't stop you and say something like, "Now, *that's* a great book . . ."

I have met artists, business people, doctors, teachers, athletes—people from different professions and possessed of seemingly different outer goals—who have attested that *Think and Grow Rich* made a concrete difference in their lives.

This is because, whatever our individual aims and desires, all motivated people share one common trait: the drive for personal excellence. This book, better than any other I know, breaks down the steps and elements to accomplishing any worthy goal.

When journalist Napoleon Hill published *Think and Grow Rich* in 1937 he had already dedicated more than twenty years of study to discovering and documenting the common traits displayed by high achievers across varying fields. Hill observed and interviewed more than five hundred exceptional people, ranging from statesmen and generals, to inventors and industrialists.

He condensed their shared traits into thirteen principles of accomplishment—and this forms the core of *Think and Grow Rich*.

This book has sold many millions of copies around the world since its first appearance—but that is not the true measure of its success. Lots of books gain popularity for a time, but go unread and sometimes unheard of within a decade or so of their publication. But *Think and Grow Rich* has, if anything, grown in influence since Hill's death in 1970. Its ideas are at the foundation of most of today's philosophies of business motivation and personal achievement.

But there is still more to Hill's book than that— and this brings us back to the little experiment proposed at the start of this preface. *Think and Grow Rich* evokes rare and deeply felt affection among many of its readers. All over America, and in other parts of the world, it is possible to run into friendly strangers who will beckon you aside for a moment to share a brief personal connection, telling you how *Think and Grow Rich* has helped them in life.

In a sense, you are about to join an informal fraternity of strivers, from a wide range of backgrounds, who have benefited from the principles in this book. When you meet them—and you will—many will welcome you with a nod and a smile, as if to say: *We've been waiting for you.*

—Mitch Horowitz

CHAPTER ONE

Desire

The First Step to Riches

In the early twentieth century a great American salesman and businessman named Edwin C. Barnes discovered how true it is that men really do *think and grow rich*.

Barnes's discovery did not come in one sitting. It came little by little, beginning with an ALL-CONSUMING DESIRE to become a business associate of inventor Thomas Edison. One of the chief characteristics of Barnes's desire was that it was *definite*. Barnes wanted to work *with* Edison—not just *for* him.

Straight off a freight train, Barnes presented himself in 1905 at Edison's New Jersey laboratory. He announced that he had come to go into business with the inventor. In speaking of their meeting years later, Edison said: "He stood there before me, looking like an ordinary tramp, but there was something in the expression of his face which conveyed the impression that he was determined to get what he had come after."

Barnes did *not* get his partnership with Edison on his first interview. But he *did* get a chance to work in the Edison offices, at a very nominal wage, doing a job that was unimportant to Edison—but *most important* to Barnes, because it gave him an opportunity to display his abilities to his future "partner."

Months passed. Nothing happened outwardly to bring Barnes any closer to his goal. But something important *was* happening in Barnes's mind. He was constantly intensifying his CHIEF DESIRE and his PLANS to become Edison's business associate.

Barnes was DETERMINED TO REMAIN READY UNTIL HE GOT THE OPPORTUNITY HE CAME FOR.

When the "big chance" arrived, it was in a different form, and from a different direction, than Barnes had expected. *That is one of the tricks of opportunity.* It has a sly habit of slipping in by the back door, and it often comes disguised as misfortune or temporary defeat. Perhaps this is why so many fail to wait for—or recognize—opportunity when it arrives.

Edison had just perfected a new device, known then as the Edison Dictating Machine. His salesmen were not enthusiastic. But Barnes saw his opportunity hidden in a strange-looking contraption that interested no one. Barnes seized the chance to sell the dictating machine, and did it so successfully that Edison gave him a contract to distribute and market it all over the world.

When Edwin C. Barnes climbed down from that freight train in Orange, New Jersey, he possessed one CONSUMING OBSESSION: to become the business associate of the great inventor. Barnes's desire was not a *hope!* It was not a *wish!* It was a keen, pulsating DESIRE, which transcended everything else. It was DEFINITE.

Wishing will not bring riches or other forms of success. But *desiring* riches with a state of mind that becomes an obsession, then planning definite ways and means to acquire riches, and backing those plans with persistence *that does not recognize failure*, will bring success.

The method by which DESIRE can be transmuted into its financial equivalent, consists of six definite, practical steps.

FIRST

Fix in your mind the *exact* amount of money you desire. It is not sufficient merely to say, "I want plenty of money." Be definite as to the amount.

SECOND
Determine exactly what you intend to give in return for the money you desire.

THIRD
Establish a definite date when you intend to *possess* the money you desire.

FOURTH
Create *a definite plan* for carrying out your desire, and begin *at once*, whether or not you are ready, to put this plan into *action*.

FIFTH
Write out a clear, concise statement of the amount of money you intend to acquire, name the time limit for its acquisition, state what you intend to give in return for the money, and describe clearly the plan through which you intend to accumulate it.

SIXTH
Read your written statement aloud, twice daily, once just before retiring at night and once after arising in the morning. AS YOU READ—SEE AND FEEL AND BELIEVE YOURSELF ALREADY IN POSSESSION OF THE MONEY.

It is especially important that you observe and follow number six. You may complain that it is impossible for you to "see yourself in possession of money" before you actually have it. Here is where a BURNING DESIRE will come to your aid. If you truly DESIRE money or another goal so keenly that your desire is an obsession, you will have no difficulty in convincing yourself that you will acquire it. The object is to want it so much and become so determined that you CONVINCE yourself you will have it. In future chapters you will learn why this is so important.

CHAPTER TWO

Faith

The Second Step to Riches

FAITH is the head chemist of the mind. When FAITH is blended with the vibration of thought, the subconscious mind instantly picks up the vibration, translates it into its spiritual equivalent, and transmits it to Infinite Intelligence, as in the case of prayer.

ALL THOUGHTS THAT HAVE BEEN EMOTIONALIZED (given feeling) AND MIXED WITH FAITH begin immediately to translate themselves into their physical equivalent.

If you have difficulty getting a grasp of just what faith is, think of it as a special form of *persistence*—one that we feel when we *know* that we have right at our backs and that helps us persevere through setbacks and temporary failure.

To develop this quality in yourself, use this five-step formula. Promise yourself to read, repeat, and abide by these steps—and write down your promise.

FIRST

I know that I have the ability to achieve the object of my DEFINITE PURPOSE in life, therefore, I *demand* of myself persistent, continuous action toward its attainment, and I here and now promise to render such action.

SECOND

I realize the dominating thoughts of my mind will eventually reproduce themselves in outward physical action, and gradually transform themselves into physical reality. Therefore, I will concentrate my thoughts for thirty minutes daily upon the task of thinking of the person I intend to become, thereby creating in my mind a clear mental picture of that person.

THIRD

I know that through the principle of auto suggestion any desire that I persistently hold in my mind will eventually seek expression through some practical means of attaining the object back of it. Therefore, I will devote ten minutes daily to demanding of myself the development of *self-confidence*.

FOURTH

I have clearly written down a description of my DEFINITE CHIEF AIM in life, and I will never stop trying until I have developed sufficient self-confidence for its attainment.

FIFTH

I fully realize that no wealth or position can long endure unless built upon truth and justice. Therefore, I will engage in no transaction which does not benefit all whom it affects. I will succeed by attracting to myself the forces I wish to use, and the cooperation of other people. I will induce others to serve me, because of my willingness to serve others. I will eliminate hatred, envy, jealousy, selfishness, and cynicism, by developing love for all humanity, because I know that a negative attitude toward others can never bring me success. I will cause others to believe in me because I will believe in them, and in myself.

I will sign my name to this formula, commit it to memory, and repeat it aloud once a day, with full FAITH that it will gradually influence my THOUGHTS and ACTIONS, so that I will become a self-reliant and successful person.

CHAPTER THREE

Auto Suggestion
The Third Step to Riches

AUTO SUGGESTION is a term that applies to all suggestions and self-administered stimuli that reach one's mind through the five senses. Stated another way: *auto suggestion is self suggestion*.

It is the agency of communication between the conscious and subconscious minds. But your subconscious mind recognizes and acts ONLY upon thoughts that have been well mixed with *emotion or feeling*. This is a fact of such importance as to warrant repetition.

When you begin to use—and keep using—the three-step program for auto suggestion in this chapter, be on the alert for hunches from your subconscious mind—and when they appear, put them into ACTION IMMEDIATELY.

FIRST

Go into some quiet spot (preferably in bed at night) where you will not be disturbed or interrupted, close your eyes, and repeat aloud (so you may hear your own words) the written statement of the amount of money you intend to accumulate, the time limit for its accumulation, and a description of the service or merchandise you intend to give in return for the money. As you carry out these instructions SEE YOURSELF ALREADY IN POSSESSION OF THE MONEY.

For example: Suppose that you intend to accumulate $50,000 by the first of January, five years hence, and that you intend to give personal services in return for the money in the capacity of a salesman. Your written statement of your purpose should be similar to the following:

"By the first day of January, I will have in my possession $50,000, which will come to me in various amounts from time to time during the interim.

"In return for this money I will give the most efficient service of which I am capable, rendering the fullest possible quantity and the best possible quality of service in the capacity of salesman of …(and describe the service or merchandise you intend to sell).

"I believe that I will have this money in my possession. My faith is so strong that I can now see this money before my eyes. I can touch it with my hands. It is now awaiting transfer to me at the time and in the proportion that I deliver the service I intend to render for it. I am awaiting a plan by which to accumulate this money, and I will follow that plan when it is received."

SECOND
Repeat this program night and morning until you can see (in your imagination) the money you intend to accumulate.

THIRD
Place a written copy of your statement where you can see it night and morning, and read it just before retiring and upon arising, until it has been memorized.

Chapter Four

Specialized Knowledge
The Fourth Step to Riches

eneral knowledge, no matter how great in quantity or variety, is of little use in accumulating money. Knowledge is only *potential* power. It becomes power only when, and if, it is organized into *definite plans of action,* and directed toward a *definite end.*

In connection with your aim, you must decide what sort of specialized knowledge you require, and the purpose for which it is needed. To a large extent, your major purpose in life, and the goal toward which you are working, will help determine what knowledge you need. With this question settled, your next move requires that you have ACCURATE INFORMATION concerning DEPENDABLE SOURCES OF KNOWLEDGE.

Look toward many high-quality sources for the knowledge you seek: people, courses, partnerships, books—look everywhere. Some of this knowledge will be free—never undervalue what is free—and some will require purchasing. Decide what knowledge you seek— and pursue it completely. The author spent more than twenty years interviewing people and studying success methods before writing this book.

Without specialized knowledge, your ideas remain mere wishes. Once you have acquired the knowledge you need, you can use your critical faculty of *imagination* to combine your IDEAS with this SPECIALIZED KNOWLEDGE, and make ORGANIZED PLANS to carry out your aims.

This is the formula for capability: *Using imagination to combine specialized knowledge with ideas and to form organized plans.*

The connecting ingredient is imagination, which we will now learn to cultivate.

CHAPTER FIVE

Imagination
The Fifth Step to Riches

The imagination is the workshop wherein are fashioned all plans created by man. The impulse, the DESIRE, is literally given shape, form, and ACTION through the aid of the imaginative faculty of the mind.

Through the medium of creative imagination, the finite mind of man has direct communication with Infinite Intelligence. Imagination is the faculty through which "hunches" and "inspirations" are reached. It is by this faculty that all basic or new ideas are handed over to man. It is through this faculty that thought vibrations from the minds of others are received. It is through this faculty that one individual may "tune in" or communicate with the subconscious minds of others.

The creative imagination works only when the conscious mind is stimulated through the emotion of a STRONG DESIRE. This is highly significant.

What's more, the creative faculty may have become weak through inaction. Your imagination becomes more alert and more receptive in proportion to its development through *use*.

After you have completed this book, return to this section and begin at once to put your imagination to work on the building of a plan, or plans, for the transmutation of *desire* into money, or your core aim. Reduce your plan to writing. The moment you complete this, you will have *definitely* given concrete form to the intangible *desire*.

This step is extremely important. When you reduce the statement of your desire, and a plan for its realization, into writing, you have actually *taken the first of* a series of steps that will enable you to covert your *thought* into its physical counterpart.

Chapter Six

Organized Planning
The Sixth Step to Riches

I t is vital that you form a DEFINITE, practical plan, or plans, to carry out your aims. You will now learn how to build plans that are *practical*, as follows:

FIRST
Ally yourself with a group of as many people as you may need for the creation and carrying out of your plan or plans for the accumulation of money—making use of the "Master Mind" principle described in a later chapter. (Compliance with this instruction is essential. Do not neglect it.)

SECOND
Before forming your "Master Mind" alliance, decide what advantages and benefits you may offer the indi-

vidual members of your group in return for their co-operation. No one will work indefinitely without some form of compensation. No intelligent person will either request or expect another to work without adequate compensation, although this may not always be in the form of money.

THIRD
Arrange to meet with the members of your "Master Mind" group at least twice a week, and more often if possible, until you have jointly perfected the necessary plan or plans for the accumulation of money.

FOURTH
Maintain *perfect harmony* between yourself and every member of your "Master Mind" group. If you fail to carry out this instruction to the letter, you may expect to meet with failure. The "Master Mind" principle *cannot* obtain where *perfect harmony* does not prevail.

Keep in mind these facts:
1. You are engaged in an undertaking of major importance to you. To be sure of success, you must have plans that are faultless.
2. You must have the advantage of the experience, education, native ability, and imagination of other

minds. This is in harmony with the methods followed by every person who has accumulated a great fortune.

Now, if the first plan you devise does not work successfully, replace it with a new plan. If this new plan fails to work, replace it, in turn, with still another, and so on, until you find a plan that *does work*. Right here is the point where the majority of men meet with failure, because of their lack of *persistence* in creating new plans to take the place of those that fail.

Remember this when your plans fail: *Temporary defeat is not permanent failure.*

No follower of this philosophy can reasonably expect to accumulate a fortune without experiencing "temporary defeat." When defeat comes, accept it as a signal that your plans are not sound, rebuild those plans, and set sail once more toward your goal.

Finally, as you are devising your plans keep in mind these Major Attributes of Leadership—traits possessed by the greatest achievers:

1. Unwavering Courage
2. Self-Control
3. A Keen Sense of Justice
4. Definiteness of Decision

5. Definiteness of Plans
6. The Habit of Doing More Than Paid For
7. A Pleasing Personality
8. Sympathy and Understanding
9. Mastery of Detail
10. Willingness to Assume Full Responsibility
11. Cooperation With Others

CHAPTER SEVEN

Decision
The Seventh Step to Riches

nalysis of several hundred people who had accumulated fortunes disclosed that *every one of them* had the habit of *reaching decisions promptly*, and of changing these decisions slowly, if and when they were changed. People who fail to accumulate money, *without exception*, have the habit of reaching decisions, if at all, very *slowly*, and of *changing these decisions quickly and often*.

What's more, the majority of people who fail to accumulate money sufficient for their needs tend to be easily influenced by the "opinions" of others. "Opinions" are the cheapest commodities on earth. Everyone has a flock of opinions ready to be wished upon anyone who will accept them. If you are influenced by "opinions" when you reach *decisions*, you will not succeed in any undertaking, much less in that of transmuting *your own desire* into money.

If you are influenced by the opinions of others, you will have no DESIRE of your own.

Keep your own counsel when you begin to put into practice the principles described here by *reaching your own decisions* and following them. Take no one into your confidence *except* the members of your "Master Mind" group, and be very sure in your selection of this group that you choose ONLY those who will be in COMPLETE SYMPATHY AND HARMONY WITH YOUR PURPOSE.

Close friends and relatives, while not meaning to, often handicap one through "opinions" and sometimes through ridicule, which is meant to be humorous. Thousands of men and women carry inferiority complexes with them throughout life, because some well-meaning but ignorant person destroyed their confidence through "opinions" or ridicule.

You have a mind of your own. USE IT and reach your own decisions. If you need facts or information from others to enable you to reach decisions, as you probably will in many instances, acquire these facts or secure the information you need quietly, without disclosing your purpose.

Those who reach DECISIONS promptly and definitely know what they want and generally get it. Leaders in every walk of life DECIDE quickly and firmly. That is the major reason why they are leaders. The world has a habit of making room for the man whose words and actions show that he knows where he is going.

Chapter Eight

Persistence
The Eighth Step to Riches

PERSITENCE is an essential factor in transmuting DESIRE into its monetary equivalent. The basis of persistence is the POWER OF WILL.

Will power and desire, when properly combined, make an irresistible pair. Men who accumulate great fortunes are generally known as cold-blooded and sometimes ruthless. Often they are misunderstood. What they have is will power, which they mix with persistence, and place at the back of their desires to *ensure* the attainment of their objectives.

Lack of persistence is one of the major causes of failure. Experience with thousands of people has proved that lack of persistence is a weakness common to the majority of men. It is a weakness that may be overcome by effort. The ease with which lack of persistence may be conquered depends *entirely* upon the INTENSITY OF ONE'S DESIRE.

In short, THERE IS NO SUBSTITUTE FOR PERSISTENCE! It cannot be supplanted by any other quality! Remember this and it will hearten you in the beginning when the going may seem difficult and slow.

Those who have cultivated the HABIT of persistence seem to enjoy insurance against failure. No matter how many times they are defeated, they finally arrive toward the top of the ladder. Sometimes it appears that there is a hidden Guide whose duty is to test men through all sorts of discouraging experiences. Those who pick themselves up after defeat and keep on trying arrive at their destination. The hidden Guide lets no one enjoy great achievement without passing the PERSISTENCE TEST.

What we DO NOT SEE, what most of us never suspect of existing, is the silent but irresistible POWER that comes to the rescue of those who fight on in the face of discouragement. If we speak of this power at all, we call it PERSISTENCE.

There are four simple steps that lead to the habit of PERSISTENCE.

1. A definite purpose backed by burning desire for its fulfillment.

2. A definite plan, expressed in continuous action.
3. A mind closed tightly against all negative and discouraging influences, including negative suggestions of relatives, friends, and acquaintances.
4. A friendly alliance with one or more persons who will encourage you to follow through with both plan and purpose.

CHAPTER NINE

The Master Mind
The Ninth Step to Riches

The "Master Mind" may be defined as: "Coordination of knowledge and effort, in a spirit of harmony, between two or more people for the attainment of a definite purpose."

No individual may hold great power without availing himself of the "Master Mind." A previous chapter supplied instructions for the creation of PLANS for the purpose of translating DESIRE into its monetary equivalent. If you carry out these instructions with PERSISTENCE and intelligence, and use discrimination in selecting your "Master Mind" group, your objective will have been halfway reached, even before you begin to recognize it.

The Master Mind brings an obvious economic advantage, by allowing you to surround yourself with the advice, counsel, and personal cooperation of a group of people who are willing to lend you wholehearted aid in a spirit of PERFECT HARMONY. But there is also a more abstract phase; it may be called the PSYCHIC PHASE.

The psychic phase of the Master Mind is more difficult to comprehend because it has reference to the spiritual forces with which the human race, as a whole, is not well acquainted. You may catch a significant suggestion from this statement: "No two minds ever come together without, thereby, creating a third invisible, intangible force which may be likened to a third mind."

The human mind is a form of energy, a part of it being spiritual in nature. When the minds of two people are coordinated in a SPIRIT OF HARMONY the spiritual units of energy of each mind form an affinity, which constitutes the "psychic" phase of the Master Mind.

Analyze the record of any man who has accumulated a great fortune, and many of those who have accumulated modest fortunes, and you will find that they have either consciously or unconsciously employed the "Master Mind."

Great power can be accumulated through no other principle!

CHAPTER TEN

Sex Transmutation
The Tenth Step to Riches

The meaning of the word "transmute" is, in simple language, "the changing or transferring of one element, or form of energy, into another." The emotion of sex brings into being a unique and powerful state of mind that can be used for extraordinary intellectual and material creative purposes.

This is accomplished through *sex transmutation*, which means the switching of the mind from thoughts of physical expression to thoughts of some other nature.

Sex is the most powerful of human desires. When driven by this desire, men develop keenness of imagination, courage, will power, persistence, and creative ability unknown to them at other times. So strong and impelling is the desire for sexual contact that men freely run the risk of life and reputation to indulge it.

When harnessed and redirected along other lines, this motivating force maintains all of its attributes of keenness of imagination, courage, etc., which may be used as powerful creative forces in literature, art, or in any other profession or calling, including, of course, the accumulation of riches.

The transmutation of sex energy calls for the exercise of will power, to be sure, but the reward is worth the effort. The desire for sexual expression is inborn and natural. The desire cannot, and should not, be submerged or eliminated. But it should be given an outlet through forms of expression that enrich the body, mind, and spirit. If not given this form of outlet, through transmutation, it will seek outlets through purely physical channels.

The emotion of sex is an "irresistible force." When driven by this emotion, men become gifted with a super power for action. Understand this truth, and you will catch the significance of the statement that sex transmutation will lift one into the status of a genius. The emotion of sex contains the secret of creative ability.

When harnessed and transmuted, this driving force is capable of lifting men to that higher sphere of thought which enables them to master the sources of worry and petty annoyance that beset their pathway on the lower plane.

The major reason why the majority of men who succeed do not begin to do so until after the ages of forty to fifty (or beyond), is their tendency to DISS-APTE their energies through over indulgence in physical expression of the emotion of sex. The majority of men *never* learn that the urge of sex has other possibilities, which far transcend in importance that of mere physical expression.

But remember, sexual energy must be *transmuted* from desire for physical contact into some *other* form of desire and action, in order to lift one to the status of a genius.

CHAPTER ELEVEN

The Subconscious Mind
The Eleventh Step to Riches

The subconscious mind is the connecting link between the finite mind of man and Infinite Intelligence. It is the intermediary through which one may draw upon the forces of Infinite Intelligence at will. It alone contains the secret process by which mental impulses are modified and changed into their spiritual equivalent. It alone is the medium through which prayer may be transmitted to the source capable of answering prayer.

I never approach the discussion of the subconscious mind without a feeling of littleness and inferiority due, perhaps, to the fact that man's entire stock of knowledge on the subject is so pitifully limited. The very fact that the subconscious mind is the medium of communication between the thinking mind of man and Infinite

Intelligence is, of itself, a thought that almost paralyzes one's reason.

After you have accepted as a reality the existence of your subconscious mind, and understand its possibilities for transmuting your DESIRES into their physical or monetary equivalent, you will understand why you have been repeatedly urged to MAKE YOUR DESIRES CLEAR, AND TO REDUCE THEM TO WRITING. You will also understand the necessity of PERSISTENCE in carrying out instructions.

The thirteen principles in this book are the stimuli with which—through practice and persistence—you acquire the ability to reach and influence your subconscious mind.

CHAPTER TWELVE

The Brain

The Twelfth Step to Riches

More than twenty years before writing this book, the author, working with the late Dr. Alexander Graham Bell and Dr. Elmer R. Gates, observed that every human brain is both a broadcasting and receiving station for the vibration of thought.

The Creative Imagination is the "receiving set" of the brain, which receives thoughts released by the brains of others. It is the agency of communication between one's conscious, or reasoning, mind, and the outer sources from which one may receive thought stimuli.

When stimulated, or "stepped up," to a high rate of vibration, the mind becomes more receptive to the vibration of thought from outside sources. This "stepping up" occurs through the positive emotions or the negative emotions. Through the emotions the vibrations of thought may be increased. This is why it is crucial that your goal have strong emotions at the back of it.

Vibrations of an exceedingly high rate are the only vibrations picked up and carried from one brain to another. Thought is energy travelling at an exceedingly high rate of vibration. Thought that has been modified or "stepped up" by any of the major emotions vibrates at a much higher rate than ordinary thought, and it is this type of thought that passes from one mind to another, through the broadcasting machinery of the human brain.

Thus, you will see that the broadcasting principle is the factor through which you mix feeling or emotion with your thoughts and pass them on to your subconscious mind, or to the minds of others.

Chapter Thirteen

The Sixth Sense
The Thirteenth Step to Riches

The thirteenth and final principle is known as the "sixth sense," through which Infinite Intelligence may and will communicate voluntarily, without any effort or demands by the individual.

After you have mastered the principles in this book, you will be prepared to accept as true a statement that may otherwise seem incredible, namely: Through the aid of the sixth sense you will be warned of impending dangers in time to avoid them, and notified of opportunities in time to embrace them.

With the development of the sixth sense, there comes to your aid, and to do your bidding, a kind of "guardian angel" who will open to you at all times the door to the Temple of Wisdom.

Whether this is a statement of truth, you will never know except by following the instructions described in this book, or some similar method.

The author is not a believer in, nor an advocate of, "miracles," for the reason that he has enough knowledge of Nature to understand that Nature *never deviates from her established laws.* Some of her laws are so incomprehensible that they produce what appear to be "miracles."

The sixth sense comes as near to being a miracle as anything I have ever experienced.

A Word About Fear

As you begin any new undertaking you are likely at one point or another to find yourself gripped by the emotion of fear.

Fear should never be bargained with or capitulated to. It takes the charm from one's personality, destroys the possibility of accurate thinking, diverts concentration of effort, masters persistence, turns the will power into nothingness, destroys ambition, beclouds the memory, and invites failure in every conceivable form. It kills love, assassinates the finer emotions of the heart, discourages friendship, and leads to sleeplessness, misery, and unhappiness.

So pernicious and destructive is the emotion of fear that it is, almost literally, worse than anything that can befall you.

If you suffer from a fear of poverty, reach a decision to get along with whatever wealth you can accumulate WITHOUT WORRY. If you fear the loss of love, reach a decision to get along without love, if that is necessary. If you experience a general sense of worry, reach a blanket decision that *nothing* life has to offer is *worth* the price of worry.

And remember: The greatest of all remedies for fear is a BURNING DESIRE FOR ACHIEVEMENT, backed by useful service to others.

NAPOLEON HILL was born in 1883 in Wise County, Virginia. He was employed as a secretary, a reporter for a local newspaper, the manager of a coalmine and a lumberyard, and attended law school, before he began working as a journalist for *Bob Taylor's Magazine,* an inspirational and general-interest journal. In 1908 the job led to his interviewing steel magnate Andrew Carnegie. The encounter changed the course of Hill's life. Carnegie believed success could be distilled into principles that anyone could follow, and urged Hill to interview the greatest industrialists, financiers, and inventors of the era to discover these principles. Hill accepted the challenge, which lasted more than twenty years and formed the building block for *Think and Grow Rich.* Hill dedicated the rest of his life to documenting and refining the principles of success. After a long career as an author, magazine publisher, lecturer, and consultant to business leaders, the motivational pioneer died in 1970 in South Carolina.

MITCH HOROWITZ, who abridged and introduced this volume, is the PEN Award-winning author of books including *Occult America* and *The Miracle Club: How Thoughts Become Reality*. *The Washington Post* says Mitch "treats esoteric ideas and movements with an even-handed intellectual studiousness that is too often lost in today's raised-voice discussions." Follow him @MitchHorowitz.

THE POWER
OF YOUR
SUBCONSCIOUS
MIND

THE POWER
OF YOUR
SUBCONSCIOUS
MIND

by Joseph Murphy

The Original Classic

Abridged and Introduced
by Mitch Horowitz

THE CONDENSED CLASSICS LIBRARY™

Contents

The Power of Thought

This may be one of the most personally important books you ever encounter. I say that not because I agree with every one of its premises or ideas. But, rather, because author and New Thought minister Joseph Murphy identifies and expands upon one immensely important and undervalued principle: *What you think dramatically affects your quality of life.*

This idea has been restated from antiquity to the present. John Milton put it this way in *Paradise Lost*: "The mind is its own place, and in it self can make a Heav'n of Hell, a Hell of Heav'n."

Murphy presents this principle as an absolute. He argues that thought governs health, finances, relationships, and all facets of life. I am personally unconvinced that *every* element of existence yields to thought alone. But within the folds of this idea—that mind is the master builder—can be found great truths. They are yours to discover, test, and benefit from. All that is required is to change how you think.

Murphy's philosophy is profoundly simple—but it is not for the weak or myopic. If you take seriously what you find in this book—and I urge you to—you will discover that redirecting your thoughts toward resiliency and constructiveness requires a lifetime of effort. But it is a task worthy of every motivated, mature person.

You will also learn that your emotions must be brought into play for any real self-change to occur. Emotion is more powerful than thought—never confuse or conflate the two. The mind says, "be satisfied with your portion"—emotion shouts, "I want more!" The mind says, "be calm"—emotion wants to run away. The mind says, "I'm happy for my neighbor"—emotion feels envy. Murphy supplies exercises to help align your emotions and thoughts in pursuit of a personal goal.

Murphy's message that *new thought means new life* has touched countless people since this book first appeared in 1963. This is not because Murphy's outlook is cloying or wishful; but because it is essentially true. We *all* feel that we should be practicing more dignified, generous, and self-respecting patterns of thought, tones of speech, and person-to-person relations. We harbor the conviction that we are *not* leading the lives we should be—that our abilities are underdeveloped, our decisions too hesitant and timorous, and our attitudes too selfish. Almost all of us sense the potential of a larger existence within us. This is a near-universal instinct.

The Power of Your Subconscious Mind is an instruction manual toward seeking that greater scale of life. Pay close attention to the book's principles, methods, and exercises. And, above all, *use them*.

It may be the most important step you ever take.

—Mitch Horowitz

CHAPTER ONE

The Treasure House
Within You

What, in your opinion, is the master secret of the ages? Atomic power? Thermonuclear energy? Interplanetary travel? No—not any of these. What, then, is the master secret? Where can one find it, and how can it be contacted and brought into action? The answer is extraordinarily simple. The secret is the marvelous, miracle-working power of your own subconscious mind.

You can bring into your life more ability, more health, more wealth, and more happiness by learning to contact and release the hidden forces of your subconscious.

As you follow the simple techniques in this book, you can gain the necessary knowledge and understanding to unlock your subconscious depths. Within them are infinite wisdom, infinite power, and infinite supply. Begin now to recognize these potentialities of your deeper mind, and they will take form in the world without.

The infinite intelligence within your subconscious can reveal to you everything you need to know at every moment, provided you are open-minded and receptive. You can receive new thoughts and ideas enabling you to bring forth new inventions, make new discoveries, or write plays and books. You can attract the ideal companion. You can acquire resources and wealth. You can move forward in abundance, security, joy, and dominion.

It is your *right* to discover this inner world of thought. Its miracle-working powers and eternal laws of life existed before you were born, before any religion or church appeared, and before the world itself came into being. It is with these thoughts that I urge you in the following chapters to lay hold of this wonderful, magical, transforming power that is your subconscious mind.

Chapter Two

How Your Mind Works

There are two levels of mind, conscious and subconscious. You think with your rational, conscious mind—and whatever you habitually think seeps down into your subconscious mind, which creates according to the nature of your thoughts.

Once the subconscious mind accepts an idea, it begins to execute it. Your subconscious does not engage in *proving* whether your thoughts are good or bad, but responds according to the *nature* of your thoughts or suggestions. If you consciously assume something is true, even though it may be false, your subconscious will accept it and proceed to bring about results that must necessarily follow.

Your conscious mind is the "watchman at the gate." Its chief function is to protect your subconscious from false impressions. You now know one of the basic laws of mind: Your subconscious is amenable to *suggestion*.

From infancy on, many of us have been given negative suggestions. Not knowing how to thwart them, we unconsciously accepted them. Here are some of the negative suggestions: "You can't." "You'll never amount to anything." "You'll fail." "You haven't got a chance." "It's no use." "It's not what you know, but who you know." "You're too old now." And so on.

If you look back, you can easily recall how parents, friends, relatives, teachers, and associates contributed to a campaign of negative suggestions. Study the things said to you, and you will discover that much of it was said to control you or instill fear in you. Check regularly on the negative suggestions that people make to you today. You do not have to be influenced by destructive suggestion.

Never say: "I can't." Overcome fear of failure by substituting the following statement: *I can do all things through the power of my subconscious mind.*

Never allow others to think for you. Choose your own thoughts, and make your own decisions. Always remember that *you have the capacity to choose.* Choose life! Choose love! Choose health! Choose happiness! Whatever your conscious mind assumes and believes, your subconscious mind accepts and brings to pass.

Chapter Three

The Miracle-Working Power
of Your Subconscious Mind

The power of your subconscious mind is enormous. It inspires you, guides you, and reveals to you names, facts, and scenes from the storehouse of memory.

Your subconscious mind never sleeps or rests. You can discover its miracle-working power by plainly stating to your subconscious prior to sleep that you wish to accomplish a certain thing. You will be delighted to find that forces within you will be released, leading to the desired answer or result.

William James, the father of American psychology, said that the power to move the world resides within your subconscious mind. Your subconscious is at one with infinite intelligence and boundless wisdom. It is fed by hidden springs. The law of life operates through it. Whatever you impress upon your subconscious, it will move heaven and earth to bring it to pass. You must, therefore, impress it with right ideas and constructive thoughts.

What is your idea or feeling about yourself right now? Every part of your being expresses that idea. Your body, vitality, finances, friends, and social status are a perfect reflection of the idea you have of yourself. What is impressed in your subconscious mind is expressed in all phases of your life.

Worry, anxiety, and fear can interfere with the normal rhythm of your heart, lungs, and other organs. Feed your subconscious mind with thoughts of harmony, health, and peace, and all the functions of your body will become normal again.

Feel the thrill of accomplishment, imagine the happy ending or solution to your problem, and what you imagine and feel will be accepted by your subconscious mind and brought to pass. The life principle will flow through you rhythmically and harmoniously as you consciously affirm: *I believe that the subconscious power that gave me this desire is now fulfilling it through me.*

Your subconscious mind can and will accomplish as much as you allow it to.

Chapter Four

Prayer and Your Subconscious Mind

In building the Golden Gate Bridge, the chief engineer understood mathematical principles, stresses, and strains. Secondly, he had a picture of the ideal bridge across the bay. The third step was his application of tried and proven methods, which were implemented until the bridge took form. Likewise, there exist techniques and methods by which your prayers are actualized.

Prayer is the formulation of an idea concerning something you wish to accomplish. Your desire *is* your prayer. It comes out of your deepest needs and it reveals what you want in life. *Blessed are they that hunger and thirst after righteousness: for they shall be filled.* That is really prayer: life's hunger and thirst for peace, harmony, health, joy, and other blessings.

We will now explore the "passing over" technique for impregnating the subconscious mind with your desire. This involves inducing the subconscious to *take over* your prayer request as handed it by the conscious mind. This *passing over* is best accomplished in a reverie-like state. Know that within your deeper mind exist infinite intelligence and infinite power. Just calmly think over what you want; and see it coming into fuller fruition from this moment forward.

Your prayer—*your mental act*—must be accepted as an image in your mind before the power of your subconscious will play upon it and make it operative. You must reach a point of *acceptance* in your mind, an unqualified and undisputed state of agreement.

This contemplation should be accompanied by a feeling of joy and restfulness in foreseeing the accomplishment of your desire. The basis for the art and science of true prayer is your knowledge and complete confidence that the movement of your conscious mind will gain a definite response from your subconscious mind.

The easiest and most obvious way to formulate an idea is to visualize it, to see it in your mind's eye as vividly as if it were alive. You can see with the naked eye only what already exists in the external world; in a similar way, that which you can visualize in your mind's eye *already exists* in the infinite realms of thought. Any picture that you have in your mind is *the substance of things hoped for and the evidence of things not seen*. What you form in your imagination is as real as any part of your body.

Your ideas and thoughts are *real*—and will one day appear in the objective world if you remain faithful to your mental image.

CHAPTER FIVE

How to Get the Results You Want

The principle reasons for failure when trying to tap your subconscious are: 1) lack of confidence, and 2) too much effort.

Many people block answers to their prayers by failing to fully comprehend the nature of their subconscious. When you know how your mind functions, you gain a measure of *confidence*. You must remember that whenever your subconscious accepts an idea, it immediately begins to execute it. It uses all its mighty resources to that end, and mobilizes all the mental and spiritual faculties of your deeper mind. This law is true for good ideas or bad. Consequently, if you use it negatively, it brings trouble, failure, and confusion. When you use it constructively, it brings guidance, freedom, and peace.

The right answer is inevitable when your thoughts are constructive and loving. The only thing you have to do to overcome failure is to get your subconscious to accept your idea or request by *feeling its reality now*, and the law of your mind will do the rest. Turn over the request with faith and confidence, and your subconscious will take over and see it through.

You will always fail to get results by trying to use *mental coercion*—your subconscious does not respond to coercion; it responds to your faith or conscious-mind acceptance. Relaxation is the key. *Easy does it.* Do not be concerned with details and means, but rest in the assured end.

Feeling is the touchstone of all subconscious demonstration. Your new idea must be *felt subjectively*, not in the future but in a finished state, as coming about now. Get the *feel* of the happy solution to your problem. Remember how you felt in the past when you solved a major problem or recovered from a serious illness. Live in this feeling, and your subconscious depths will bring it to pass.

Chapter Six

How to Use Your Subconscious Mind for Wealth

Wealth is a subconscious conviction on the part of the individual. You will not become a millionaire by saying, "I am a millionaire, I am a millionaire." Rather, you will *grow into a wealth consciousness* by building into your mentality the idea of wealth and abundance.

Perhaps you are saying to yourself now, "I need wealth and success." Follow these steps: Repeat for about five minutes to yourself three or four times a day, "Wealth—Success." These words have tremendous power. They represent the inner power of the subconscious. Anchor your mind on this substantial power within you; then corresponding conditions and circumstances will be manifested in your life.

Again, you are not merely saying, "I am wealthy." You are dwelling on real powers within you. There is no conflict in the mind when you say, "Wealth." Furthermore, the *feeling* of wealth will well up within you as you dwell on the idea of wealth.

I have talked to many people during the past thirty-five years whose usual complaint is: "I have said for weeks and months, 'I am wealthy, I am prosperous,' and nothing has happened." I discovered that when they said, "I am prosperous, I am wealthy," they felt within that they were lying to themselves. One man told me, "I have affirmed that I am prosperous until I am tired. Things are now worse. I knew when I made that statement that it was obviously not true." His statements were rejected by the conscious mind, and the very opposite of what he outwardly affirmed was made manifest.

Your affirmation succeeds best when it is specific and when it does not produce a mental conflict or argument; hence, the statements made by this man made matters worse because they suggested his lack. Your subconscious mind accepts what you really feel to be true, not just idle words or statements.

Here is the ideal way to overcome this conflict. Make this statement frequently, particularly prior to sleep: *By day and by night I am being prospered in all of my interests.* This affirmation will not arouse any argument because it does not contradict your subconscious mind's impression of financial lack.

Many people tell themselves, "I deserve a higher salary." I believe that most people are, in fact, underpaid. One reason why many people do not have more money is that they are silently or openly condemning it. They call money "filthy lucre" or say "love of money is the root of all evil." Another reason they do not prosper is that they have a sneaky subconscious feeling that there is some virtue in poverty. This subconscious pattern may be due to early childhood training, superstition, or a mistaken interpretation of Scripture

Cleanse your mind of all conflicting beliefs about money. Do not regard money as evil or filthy. If you do, you cause it to take wings and fly away from you. You lose what you condemn.

At the same time, do not make a god of money. It is only a symbol. Remember that the real riches are in your mind. You are here to lead a balanced life—and that includes acquiring all the money you need.

There is one emotion that causes lack of wealth in the lives of many. Most people learn this the hard way. It is envy. To entertain envious thoughts is devastating; it places you in a negative position in which wealth flows *from* you rather than *to* you. If you are ever annoyed or irritated by the prosperity of another, claim immediately that you truly wish him greater wealth in every possible way. This will neutralize your negative thoughts, and cause an ever-greater measure of wealth to flow to you.

Chapter Seven

Your Subconscious Mind as a Partner in Career Success

Let us discuss three steps to success. The first step is to discover the thing you love to do, and then do it. Success is in loving your work.

Some may say, "How can I put the first step into operation? I do not know what I should do." In such a case, pray for guidance as follows: *The infinite intelligence of my subconscious mind reveals to me my true place in life.* Repeat this prayer quietly, positively, and lovingly to your deeper mind. As you persist with faith and confidence, the answer will come to you as a feeling, a hunch, or a tendency in a certain direction. It will come to you clearly and in peace, as an inner awareness.

The second step to success is to specialize in some particular branch of work, and to know more about it than anyone else. For example, if a young man chooses chemistry as his profession, he should concentrate on one of the many branches in that field. He should give all of his time and attention to his chosen specialty. He should become sufficiently enthusiastic to know all there is about it; if possible, he should know more than anyone else.

The third step is the most important. You must be certain that the thing you want to do does not build your success only. *Your desire must not be selfish; it must benefit humanity.* The path of a complete circuit must be formed. In other words, your idea must go forth with the purpose of blessing or serving the world. It will then come back to you pressed down, shaken together, and running over. If it is to benefit you alone, the circle or circuit is not formed.

A successful person loves his work and expresses himself fully. True success is contingent upon a higher ideal than mere accumulation of riches. The person of success is one who possesses great psychological and spiritual understanding, and whose work benefits others.

Chapter Eight

The Inventiveness of Your Subconscious Mind

Nikola Tesla was a brilliant electrical scientist who brought forth amazing inventions in the late-nineteenth and early twentieth centuries. When an idea for a new invention entered Tesla's mind, he would build it up in his imagination, knowing that his subconscious would construct and reveal to his conscious mind all the parts needed for its manufacture. Through quietly contemplating every possible improvement, he spent no time in correcting defects, and was able to give technicians perfect plans for the product.

"Invariably," he said, "my device works as I imagined it should. In twenty years there has not been a single exception."

When you have what you term "a difficult decision" to make, or when you fail to see the solution to a problem, begin at once to think constructively about it. If you are fearful and worried, you are not really thinking. True thinking is free from fear.

Here is a simple technique to receive inner guidance on any subject: Quiet the mind and still the body. Go to a quiet place where you won't be disturbed—preferably lying on a bed, sofa, or in a recliner. Mobilize your attention; focus your thoughts on the solution to the problem. Try to solve it with your conscious mind. Think how happy you would be with the perfect solution. Sense the feeling you would have if the right answer were yours now. Let your mind play with this mood in a relaxed way; then drop off to sleep. When you awaken, and do not have the answer, get busy about something else. When you are preoccupied with something else, the answer will probably come into your mind like toast pops from out of a toaster.

The secret of guidance or right action is to mentally devote yourself to the right answer, until you find its response in you. The response is a feeling, an inner awareness, and an overpowering hunch whereby *you know that you know*. In such cases, you have used the infinite power of your subconscious to the point where *it begins to use you*. You cannot fail or make a false step while operating under the subconscious wisdom within you.

CHAPTER NINE

Your Subconscious Mind and Marital Problems

Recently a young couple, married for only a few months, was seeking a divorce. I discovered that the young man had a constant fear that his wife would leave him. He expected rejection, and he believed that she would be unfaithful. These thoughts haunted him and became an obsession. His mental attitude was one of separation and suspicion. His own feeling of loss and separation operated through the relationship. This brought about a condition in accordance with the mental pattern behind it.

His wife left home and asked for a divorce, which is what he feared and believed would happen.

Divorce occurs first in the mind; the legal proceedings follow. These two young people were full of resentment, fear, suspicion, and anger. These attitudes weaken and debilitate the whole being. The couple began to realize what they had been doing with their minds. These two people returned together at my suggestion and experimented with *prayer therapy*, a method we will learn.

Each one practiced radiating to the other love, peace, harmony, health, and good will. They alternated in reading the Psalms every night. Their marriage began growing more beautiful every day.

Now, divorce is an individual problem. It cannot be generalized. In some cases, no marriage should have occurred to begin with. In other cases, divorce is not the solution. Divorce may be right for one person and wrong for another. A divorced woman may be far more sincere and noble than many of her married sisters, who are perhaps living a lie.

For couples that wish to *stay together* the solution is to *pray together*. Here is a three-step program in prayer therapy.

FIRST

Never carry over from one day to another accumulated irritations arising from little disappointments. Forgive each other for any sharpness before you retire at night. The moment you awaken, claim infinite intelligence is guiding you in all ways. Send out thoughts of peace, harmony, and love to your partner, to all family members, and to the entire world.

SECOND
Say grace at breakfast. Give thanks for the wonderful food, for your abundance, and for all your blessings. Make sure that no problems, worries, or arguments enter into the table conversation; the same applies at dinnertime. Say to your partner, "I appreciate all you are doing, and I radiate love and good will to you all day long."

THIRD
Spouses should alternate in praying each night. Do not take your marriage partner for granted. Show your appreciation and love. Think appreciation and good will, rather than condemnation, criticism, and nagging. Before going to sleep read the 23rd, 27th, and 91st Psalms; the 11th chapter of Hebrews; the 13th chapter of I Corinthians; and other great texts of the Bible.

As you practice these steps, your marriage will grow more blessed through the years.

CHAPTER TEN

Your Subconscious Mind and Happiness

There is a phrase in the Bible: *Choose ye this day whom ye will serve.*

You have the freedom to *choose happiness.* This may seem extraordinarily simple—and it is. Perhaps this is why so many people stumble over the way to happiness; they do not see the simplicity of the key to happiness. The great things of life are simple, dynamic, and creative.

St. Paul reveals how you can think your way into a life of dynamic power and happiness in these words: *Finally, brethren, whatsoever things are true, whatsoever things are honest, whatsoever things are just, whatsoever things are pure, whatsoever things are lovely, whatsoever things are of good report; if there be any virtue, and if there be any praise, think on these things.* (Philippians 4:8)

There is one very important point about being happy. You must sincerely *desire* to be happy. Some people have been depressed, dejected, and unhappy for so long that when they are suddenly made happy by some joyous news they actually feel uncomfortable. They have become so accustomed to the old mental patterns that they do not feel at home being happy. They long for the familiar depressed state.

Begin now to choose happiness. Here is how: When you open your eyes in the morning, say to yourself: *Divine order takes charge of my life today and every day. All things work together for good for me today. This is a new and wonderful day for me. There will never be another day like this one. I am divinely guided all day long, and whatever I do will prosper. Divine love surrounds me, enfolds me, and enwraps me, and I go forth in peace. Whenever my attention wanders away from what is good and constructive, I will immediately bring it back to the contemplation of that which is lovely and of good report. I am a spiritual and mental magnet attracting to myself all things that bless and prosper me. I am going to be a wonderful success in all my undertakings today. I am definitely going to be happy all day long.*

Start each day in this manner; you will then be choosing happiness.

Chapter Eleven

Your Subconscious Mind and Harmonious Relationships

Matthew 7:12 says, *All things whatsoever ye would that men should do unto you, do ye even so to them.*

This passage has outer and inner meanings. We are interested in its inner meaning, which is: As you would that men should *think* about you, think about them. As you would that men should *feel* about you, feel about them. As you would want men to *act* toward you, act toward them.

For example, you may be polite and courteous to someone in your office, but inside you are critical and resentful. Such negative thoughts are highly destructive to you. You are actually taking mental poisons, which rob you of enthusiasm, strength, guidance, and good will. These negative thoughts and emotions sink into your subconscious, and cause you all kinds of difficulties and maladies.

Matthew 7:1-2 says, *Judge not, that ye not be judged. For with what judgment ye judge, ye shall be judged; and with what measure ye shall mete, it shall be measured to you again.*

The study and application of these verses, and their inner truth, provides the key to harmonious relations. To judge is to think, to reach a mental verdict or conclusion in your mind. Your thoughts are creative, therefore, you actually create in your own experience what you think and feel about another person. It is also true that the suggestion you give to another, you give to yourself.

Now, there *are* difficult people in the world who are twisted and distorted mentally. They are malconditioned. Many are mental delinquents, argumentative, uncooperative, cantankerous, and cynical. They are sick psychologically. Many people have deformed and distorted minds, probably warped during childhood. Many have congenital deformities. You would not condemn a person who had tuberculosis, nor should you condemn someone who is mentally ill. You should have compassion and understanding. *To understand all is to forgive all.*

At the same time, do not permit people to take advantage of you and gain their point by temper tantrums, crying jags, or so-called heart attacks. These people are dictators who try to enslave you and make you do their bidding. Be firm but kind, and refuse to yield. *Appeasement never wins.* You are here to fulfill your ideal and to remain true to the eternal verities and spiritual values of life.

Give no one the power to deflect you from your goal, your aim in life, which is to express your hidden talents to the world, to serve humanity, and to reveal more and more of God's wisdom, truth, and beauty. Know definitely that whatever contributes to your peace, happiness, and fulfillment must, of necessity, bless all who walk the earth. The harmony of the part is the harmony of the whole, for the whole is in the part, and the part in the whole.

How Your Subconscious Mind Removes Mental Blocks

A young man asked Socrates how he could get wisdom. Socrates replied, "Come with me." He took the lad to a river, pushed the boy's head under the water, held it there until the boy was gasping for air, then relaxed and released his head. When the boy regained his composure, the teacher asked, "What did you desire most when you were under water?"

"I wanted air," said the boy.

Socrates told him, "When you want wisdom as much as you wanted air, you will receive it."

Likewise, when you possess an intense desire to overcome any block or addiction, and you reach a clear-cut decision that there is a way out, and that is the course you wish to follow, then victory and triumph are assured.

If you are an alcoholic or drug addict, begin by admitting it. Do not dodge the issue. Many people remain alcoholics because they refuse to admit it. If you have a burning desire to free yourself from any destructive habit, you are fifty-one percent healed. When you have a greater desire to give up a habit than to continue it, you will gain complete freedom.

Whatever thought you anchor the mind upon, the mind magnifies. If you engage the mind on the concept of freedom from habit and peace of mind, you generate feelings that gradually emotionalize the concept of freedom and peace. Whatever idea you emotionalize is accepted by your subconscious and brought to pass.

Use these steps to help cope with addiction:

FIRST
Get still; quiet the wheels of the mind. Enter into a sleepy, drowsy state. In this relaxed, peaceful, receptive state you are preparing for the second step.

SECOND
Take a brief phrase, which can readily be graven on the memory, and repeat it over and over as a lullaby. Use the phrase: *Sobriety and peace of mind are mine now, and I give thanks.* To prevent the mind from wandering, repeat the phrase aloud or sketch its pronunciation with

your lips and tongue as you say it mentally. This helps its entry into your subconscious. Do this for five minutes or more. You will find a deep emotional response.

THIRD

Just before going to sleep, imagine a friend or loved one in front of you. Your eyes closed, you are relaxed and at peace. The loved one or friend is subjectively present, and is saying to you, "Congratulations!" You see the smile; you hear the voice. You mentally touch the hand; it is all vivid and real. The word "congratulations" implies *complete freedom*. Hear it over and over until you get the subconscious reaction that satisfies.

CHAPTER THIRTEEN

How to Stay
Young in Spirit Forever

Your subconscious never grows old. It is part of the universal mind of God, which was never born and will never die.

Patience, kindness, veracity, humility, good will, harmony, and brotherly love are eternal attributes, which never age. If you continue to generate these qualities, you will remain young in spirit.

During my many years of public life, I have studied the careers of famous people who have continued their productivity well beyond the normal span of life. Some achieved their greatness in old age. I have also met and known countless individuals of no prominence who, in their lesser sphere, belong to those hardy mortals who have proven that old age of itself does not destroy the creative powers of the mind and body.

My father learned French at sixty-five, and became an authority on it at seventy. He made a study of Gaelic when he was over sixty, and became a well-regarded teacher of the subject. He assisted my sister in a school of higher learning and continued to do so until he passed away at ninety-nine. His mind was as clear at ninety-nine as it was at twenty. Moreover, his handwriting and reasoning powers improved with age.

A Hollywood screenwriter told me that he had to write scripts that would cater to the twelve-year-old mind. This is a tragic state of affairs if the great masses of people are expected to be emotionally and spiritually mature. It means the emphasis is placed on youth in spite of how youth stands for inexperience, lack of discernment, and hasty judgment.

Old age really means the contemplation of the truths of God from the highest standpoint. Realize that you are on an endless journey, a series of important steps in the ceaseless, tireless, endless ocean of life. Then, with the Psalmist, you will say, *They shall still bring forth fruit in old age; they shall be fat and flourishing.* (Psalm 92:14)

You are a child of Infinite Life, which knows no end, a child of Eternity.

JOSEPH MURPHY was born in 1898 on the southern coast of Ireland. Raised in a devout Catholic family, Murphy had planned on joining the priesthood. As young man he instead relocated to America to make his career as a chemist and druggist. After running a pharmacy counter at New York's Algonquin Hotel, Murphy began studying mystical and metaphysical ideas. In the 1940s he became a popular New Thought minister and writer. Murphy wrote prolifically on the autosuggestive and mystical faculties of the human mind. He became widely known for his metaphysical classic, *The Power of Your Subconscious Mind*, which has sold millions of copies since it first appeared in 1963. Considered one of the pioneering voices of New Thought and affirmative-thinking philosophy, Murphy died in Laguna Hills, California, in 1981.

MITCH HOROWITZ, who abridged and introduced this volume, is the PEN Award-winning author of books including *Occult America* and *The Miracle Club: How Thoughts Become Reality*. *The Washington Post* says Mitch "treats esoteric ideas and movements with an even-handed intellectual studiousness that is too often lost in today's raised-voice discussions." Follow him @MitchHorowitz.

PUBLIC SPEAKING TO WIN!

PUBLIC
SPEAKING
TO WIN!

by Dale Carnegie

The Original Formula to
Speaking with Power

Abridged and Introduced
by Mitch Horowitz

Contents

The Power of What You Say

Nearly everything worth accomplishing in life comes down to communication. Your ability to sway others, win support, gain resources, succeed in your work, and correct injustice rests on your power of persuasion.

Even in our social-media age, the spoken word remains paramount. Candidates are elected because of what they say and how. Court trials hang on spoken testimony. Job interviews are face-to-face encounters. The same holds true for pitches to clients, donors, investors, customers, and financial backers. If you are seeking a career as a teacher, military officer, actor, broadcaster, or leader in any almost any field, your speaking ability is vital to your success.

Strikingly little has changed in human relations since Dale Carnegie wrote this guide to speaking in 1926, a decade before he gained international fame as the author of *How to Win Friends and Influence People*. When Carnegie produced this book he was making his living as the teacher of a popular seminar on public speaking. Carnegie had begun teaching his methods in 1912 at a YMCA in New York City. Requests for his course came in from around the country. By the mid-1930s, *Ripley's Believe-It-Or-Not* anointed Carnegie the king of public speaking with a cartoon reporting that he had personally critiqued 150,000 speeches.

Whether this is exaggerated, Carnegie's guide-book remains probably the best ever on how to speak with conviction and power. The book shows how to capture people's attention and win their confidence, whether you are speaking at a local club, a national sales conference, or in front of a class. But, as you will discover, this book delivers far more than instructions on how to give a good talk. Its greater value is that it teaches how to communicate effectively in virtually every sphere of life, on any occasion, and on behalf of any aim or purpose.

If you are a salesman, the book will help you will sell more. If you are a writer or editor, you will learn to better connect with readers. If you are an activist, you will find new ways to rally people to your cause.

What is the secret of Carnegie's formula? It comes down to three principles.

First, have an airtight knowledge of your subject—
know more than you need.

Second, when speaking, use plain language, personal examples, and tell stories of people.

Third, and finally, appeal to your listeners' sense
of self-interest: We all crave safety, success, health, and
prosperity. We also have a yearning for justice and fair-
ness. Speak on these points, and you will likely bring
people to your side.

Unless you are one of a very few naturally gifted
speakers, implementing these simple guidelines requires
persistence, inspiration, and strategy. You will find all of
that—and more—in this book.

Carnegie's methods will bring you increased power.
Use it for good ends.

—Mitch Horowitz

CHAPTER ONE

Developing Courage and Self-Confidence

Thousands of businessmen have taken my public-speaking courses. The vast majority have told me the same thing: "When I am called upon to stand up and speak, I become so self-conscious, so frightened, that I can't think clearly, can't concentrate, and can't remember what I wanted to say. I want to gain self-confidence, poise, and the ability to think on my feet."

Gaining self-confidence and courage, and the ability to think calmly and clearly while talking to a group, is not nearly as difficult as most imagine. It is not a gift bestowed by Providence. It is like the ability to play golf. Anyone can develop his own latent capacity, if he has sufficient desire to do so.

Rather than being frightened to speak publicly, you ought to think and speak *better* in front of a group. Their presence ought to lift and stir you. Many speakers will tell you that an audience is a stimulus, an inspiration that drives their brains to function more clearly, more keenly. At such times, thoughts, facts, and ideas that they did not know they possessed come to them. This will probably be your experience if you practice and persevere.

In order to get the most from this book, and to get it quickly, four things are essential:

FIRST

Start with a persistent desire. This is of far greater importance than you may realize. If I could look into your heart and mind right now, and ascertain the depth of your desires, I could foretell with near-certainty the swiftness of your progress. If your desire is pale and flabby, your achievements will be the same. But if you go after this subject with persistence, nothing will defeat you. Therefore, arouse your enthusiasm for this study. Think of what additional self-confidence and speaking ability will mean to you. Think of what it may mean in profits. Think of what it may mean socially—of the friends it will bring, of the increase of your personal influence, of the leadership it will give you.

SECOND

Know thoroughly what you intend to talk about. Unless a speaker has thought out and planned what he is going to say, he can't feel very comfortable when facing his auditors. An unprepared speaker *ought* to be self-conscious—and ought to be ashamed of his negligence.

THIRD

Act confident. "To feel brave," advises philosopher William James, "act as if we *were* brave, use all our will to that end, and a courage-fit will very likely replace the fit of fear." To develop courage when facing an audience, act as if you already have it. Unless you are prepared, of course, all the acting in the world will amount to little.

FOURTH

Practice! Practice! Practice! This is the most vital point of all. The first way, the last way, the never-failing way to overcome fear and develop self-confidence in speaking is—to speak. The whole matter finally simmers down to one essential: *practice.*

Chapter Two

Self-Confidence Through Preparation

It has been my professional duty, as well as my pleasure, to listen to and criticize approximately six thousand speeches a year. Most were made by ordinary businesspeople. If that experience has engraved one thing on my mind it is this: the urgent necessity of preparing a talk before one starts to make it, and of having something clear and definite to say.

Aren't you unconsciously drawn to a speaker who you feel has a real message, which he zealously desires to communicate? That is half the secret of speaking. When a speaker is in that kind of mental and emotional state he will discover a significant fact: his talk almost makes itself. A well-prepared speech is already nine-tenths delivered. The one fatal mistake is neglecting to prepare. "Perfect love," wrote the apostle John, "casteth out fear." So does perfect preparation.

What is preparation? Reading a book? That is one kind, but not the best. Reading may help; but if one attempts to lift a lot of "canned" thoughts out of a book and give them out as his own, the whole performance will be lacking.

Does preparation mean pulling together some faultless phrases, written down or memorized? No. Does it mean assembling a few casual thoughts that really convey very little to you personally? Not at all.

It means assembling *your* thoughts, *your* ideas, *your* convictions, *your* urges. You have them everyday of your life. They swarm through your dreams. Your whole existence has been filled with feelings and experiences. These things are lying deep in your subconscious as thick as pebbles on the seashore. Preparation means thinking, brooding, recalling, selecting the ones that speak to you most, polishing them, working them into a pattern, a mosaic of your own. That doesn't sound so difficult, does it? It isn't. It just requires a little concentration and thinking to a purpose.

What topics should you speak on? Anything that truly interests you. Ask yourself all possible questions concerning your topic. For example, if you are to speak on divorce, ask yourself what causes divorce, what are the effects economically, socially, domestically? Should we have uniform divorce laws? Should divorce be more difficult? Easier?

When preparing a speech, assemble a hundred thoughts, and discard ninety. Collect more material than there is any possibility of using. Get it for that additional confidence it will give you, for that sureness of touch. Get it for the effect it will have on your mind and heart and whole manner of speaking. That is a basic factor of preparation—yet most speakers constantly ignore it.

You must practice your speaking. If you stand up and think clearly and keep going for two or three minutes, that is a perfect way to practice delivering a talk. Try this a few times. What you can do first on a small scale you can do later on a large scale.

When making your practice talk, do not attempt to tell us everything in three minutes. It can't be done. Take one, and only one, phase of your topic: expand and enlarge that. For example, you can tell us how you came to be in your particular business or profession. Was it due to accident or choice? Relate your early struggles, your defeats, your hopes, and your triumphs. Give us a human-interest narrative, a real-life picture based on first-hand experience. The truthful, inside story of almost anyone's life—if told modestly and without egotism—is sure-fire speech material.

Many wonder if they should use notes while speaking. As a listener, don't notes destroy about fifty percent of your interest in a talk? Notes prevent, or at least render difficult, a very precious intimacy that ought to exist between the speaker and the audience. They create an air of artificiality. They restrain an audience from feeling that a speaker has confidence, spontaneity, and power.

Make notes during your preparation—elaborate ones, profuse ones. You may wish to refer to them when you are practicing your talk alone. You may possibly feel more comfortable if you have them stored away in your pocket when facing an audience. But they should be emergency tools, used only in case of a total wreck.

If you *must* use notes while speaking, make them extremely brief and write them in large letters on an ample sheet of paper. Then arrive early where you are speaking and discretely place your notes on the lectern, or conceal them behind books on a table. Glance at them if you must, but be brief.

In a few limited instances it may be wise to use notes. Some people during their first few talks are so nervous that they are unable to remember what they wanted to say. In such cases, it is fine to hold a few very condensed notes in your hands.

Get comfortable with your talk. After you have thought it out and arranged it, practice it silently as you walk along the street. Also get off somewhere by yourself and go over it from beginning to end, using gestures, letting yourself go. Imagine that you are addressing a real audience. The more of this you do, the more comfortable you will feel when the time comes to deliver your talk.

CHAPTER THREE

Keeping Your Audience Awake

What is the secret of success? "Nothing great," said Ralph Waldo Emerson, "was ever achieved without enthusiasm." This quality is the most effective, most important factor in advertising, selling goods, and getting things done.

I once put considerable reliance on the *rules* of public speaking. But with the passing of years I have come to put more and more faith in the *spirit* of speaking.

Remember always that every time we speak we determine the attitude of our listeners. If we are lackadaisical, they will be lackadaisical. If we are reserved, they will be reserved. If we are only mildly concerned, they will be only mildly concerned. But if we are deadly in earnest about what we say, and if we say it with feeling and spontaneity and force and conviction, they cannot keep from catching our spirit to a degree.

So, to feel earnest and enthusiastic, stand up and *act* in earnest and *be* enthusiastic. Stop leaning against the table. Stand tall. Stand still. Don't rock back and forth. Don't bob up and down. Don't shift your weight from one foot to the other and back again. In short, don't make a lot of nervous movements. They proclaim your lack of ease and self-possession. Control yourself physically. It conveys a sense of poise and power. Fill your lungs with oxygen. Look straight at your audience. Look at them as if you have something urgent to say. Look at them with the confidence and courage of a teacher, for you *are* a teacher, and they are there to hear you and to be taught.

Use emphatic gestures. Never mind, just now, whether they are beautiful or graceful. Think only of making them forceful and spontaneous. Make them now, not for the sense they will convey to others, but for what they will do for *you*. And they will do wonders. Even if you are speaking to a radio audience, *gesture, gesture.* Your gestures won't, of course, be visible to the hearers, but the result of your gestures will be audible to them. They will give increased aliveness and energy to your tone.

I have made a special study of Abraham Lincoln as a public speaker. He is perhaps the most loved man

America has ever produced; and unquestionably he delivered some of America's greatest speeches. Although he was a genius in some ways, I am inclined to believe that his power with audiences was due, in large measure, to his sympathy and honesty and goodness. He loved people. "His heart," said his wife, "is as large as his arms are long." He was Christlike.

The finest thing in speaking is neither physical nor mental. It is spiritual. Jesus loved men and their hearts burned within them as He talked with them by the way. If you want a splendid text on public speaking, read your New Testament.

CHAPTER FOUR

The Secret of Good Delivery

We are often told to be natural, to be ourselves. But the same society that gives this advice often bleeds naturalness out of us by imposing all kinds of preconceptions of just what "naturalness" ought to be.

The problem of teaching or training people in delivery is not one of superimposing additional characteristics; it is largely one of removing impediments, of freeing people, of getting them to speak, albeit with a different vocabulary and judgment, as they did when they were four years old.

As you practice, if you find yourself talking in a stilted manner, pause and say sharply to yourself mentally: "What is wrong? Wake up. Be human." In the end, even the matter of delivery comes back to a point that has already been emphasized: namely, *put your heart in your talks.*

Here are four things that all of us do unconsciously and naturally in conversation. You should do them when speaking in public.

1. Stress the important words in a sentence and subordinate the unimportant ones. When you speak conversationally you naturally give emphasis to keywords, such as *ambition, affliction,* and *skyscraper.* But not to unimportant words, such as *the, and,* or *but.*

2. Allow the pitch of your voice to flow up and down the scale from high to low and back again—as the pitch of a little child does when speaking.

3. Vary your rate of speaking, running rapidly over the unimportant words, spending more time on the ones you wish to make stand out.

4. And, finally, pause before and after your important ideas.

This is exactly how you speak to your friends, coworkers, or spouse—and it is how you should address an audience.

CHAPTER FIVE

Platform Presence and Personality

*P*ersonality—with the exception of *preparation* and *ideas*—is probably the most important factor in public speaking. But personality is a vague and elusive thing. It is the whole combination of the man: the physical, the spiritual, the mental; his traits, his predilections, his tendencies, his temperament, his cast of mind, his vigor, his experience, his training, his life.

If you wish to make the most of your individuality, go before your audience well rested. A tired person is not magnetic or attractive. When you have to make an important talk, beware of your hunger. Eat as sparingly as a saint. Do nothing to dull your senses or energy.

To maintain high spirits in the room, make sure that your audience—whether it is large or small—is grouped closely together. No audience will be easily moved when it is scattered. Nothing so dampens enthusiasm as wide, open spaces and empty chairs between the listeners.

If you are going to talk to a small group, choose a small room. Better to pack the aisles of a small place than to have people dispersed through the lonely, deadening spaces of a large hall. If your hearers are scattered, ask them to move down front and be seated near you. Insist on this before you start speaking.

Unless the audience is a fairly large one, and there is a real reason, a necessity, for you to stand on a platform, do not do so. Get down on the same level with your listeners. Stand near them. Break up all formality. Get an intimate contact. Make the thing conversational.

Take a deep breath. Look over your audience for a moment. If there is a noise or disturbance, pause until it quiets down. Hold your chest high. But why wait until you get before an audience to do this? Do it daily in private life. Then you will do it unconsciously in public.

And what shall you do with your hands? Forget them. If they fall naturally to your sides, that is ideal. And this returns us to the much-abused question of gesture. A man's gestures, like his toothbrush, should be very personal things. As all of us are different, our gestures will be individual if only we act natural. No two people should be drilled to gesture in precisely the same fashion.

I can't give you rules for gesturing—and neither can anyone else. For everything depends on the temperament of the speaker, upon his preparation, his enthusiasm, his personality, the subject, the audience, the occasion. Above all, be truthful; be comfortable; be yourself.

Chapter Six

How to Open a Talk

For some unfortunate reason, the novice often feels that he ought to be funny as a speaker. So he is inclined to open with a humorous story, especially if the occasion is an after-dinner affair. The chances are his stories don't "click." In the immortal language of Hamlet, they prove "weary, stale, flat, and unprofitable."

In the difficult realm of speechmaking, what is more difficult, more rare, than the ability to make an audience laugh? Remember, it is seldom the story that is funny. It is *the way it is told* that makes it a success. Ninety-nine people out of a hundred will fail woefully with the identical stories that made Mark Twain famous.

The second egregious blunder that the beginner is likely to make in his opening is this: He apologizes. "I am no speaker . . . I am not prepared to talk . . . I have nothing to say . . ." Don't! Don't! Why insult your audience by suggesting that you did not think them worth preparing for, that just any old thing you happened to have on the fire would be good enough to serve them? We don't want to hear your apologies. We are there to be informed and interested—to be *interested*, remember that.

Arouse your audience's curiosity with your first sentence—and you have their attention. An article in *The Saturday Evening Post* entitled "With the Gangsters," began: "Are gangsters really organized? As a rule they are. How?" With ten words the writer announced his subject, told you something about it, and aroused your curiosity.

Everyone who aspires to speak in public ought to study the techniques that magazine writers use to immediately hook the reader's interest. You can learn far more from them about how to open a speech than you can by studying collections of speeches.

CHAPTER SEVEN

How to Close a Talk

If you want to know how to end a speech, you can do no better than study the close of Lincoln's Second Inaugural:

> *With malice toward none, with charity for all, with firmness in the right as God gives us to see the right, let us strive on to finish the work we are in, to bind up the nation's wounds, to care for him who shall have borne the battle and for his widow and his orphan, to do all which may achieve and cherish a just and lasting peace among ourselves and with all nations.*

You have just encountered what is, in my opinion, the most beautiful speech ending ever delivered. But you are not going to deliver immortal pronouncements as president in Washington or prime minister in Ottawa.

Your problem, perhaps, will be how to close a simple talk before a group of businessmen. How shall you set about it? Here are some suggestions.

FIRST

Even in a short talk of three to five minutes, a speaker is very apt to cover so much ground that at the close his listeners are a little hazy about all his main points. Some anonymous Irish politician is reported to have given this famous recipe for making a speech: "First, tell them what you are going to tell them; then, tell them; then, tell them what you told them." It is often highly advisable to "tell them what you told them." Briefly, of course, speedily—a mere outline, a summary.

SECOND

Try closing with a poetical quotation. If you can get a proper verse of poetry for your closing, it is almost ideal. It will give the desired flavor. It will give dignity. It will give individuality. It will give beauty. A choice Biblical quotation often has a profound effect.

THIRD

Build to a climax. The climax is a popular way of ending. It is often difficult to manage and is not an ending for all speakers or all subjects. But, when well done, it is excellent. It works up to a crest, a peak, getting stronger sentence by sentence. It often means ending with a tribute to someone or something, or an appeal for action—a topic we will cover in a future chapter.

CHAPTER EIGHT

How to Make
Your Meaning Clear

Napoleon's most emphatic instruction to his secretaries was: "Be clear! Be clear!"

When the disciples asked Christ why He taught the public by parables, He answered: "Because they seeing, see not; and hearing, hear not; neither do they understand."

And when you talk about a subject strange to your hearers, can you hope that they will understand you any more readily than people understood the Master?

Hardly. So what can we do about it? What did he do? He solved it in the most simple and natural manner imaginable: described the things people did not know by likening them to things they did know. The kingdom of Heaven . . . what would it be like?

"The kingdom of Heaven is like unto leaven . . . The kingdom of Heaven is like unto a merchant seeking goodly pearls . . . The kingdom of Heaven is like unto a net that was cast into the sea."

That was lucid; they could understand that. The housewives in the audience were using leaven every week; the fishermen were casting their nets into the sea daily; the merchants were dealing in pearls.

I once heard a lecturer on Alaska who failed, in many places, to be either clear or interesting because he neglected to talk in terms of what his audience knew. He told us, for example, that Alaska had a gross area of 590,804 miles.

Half-a-million square miles—what does that mean to the average person? Precious little. He is not used to thinking in square miles. They conjure up no mental picture. He does not have any idea whether half-a-million square miles are approximately the size of Maine or Texas. Suppose the speaker had said that the coastline of Alaska and its islands is longer than the distance around the globe, and that its area more than equals the combined areas of Vermont, New Hampshire, Maine, Massachusetts, Rhode Island, Connecticut, New York, New Jersey, Pennsylvania, Delaware, Maryland, West Virginia, North Carolina, South Carolina, Georgia, Florida, Mississippi, and Tennessee. Would that not give everyone a fairly clear conception of the area of Alaska?

If you belong to a profession that does technical work—if you are a lawyer, physician, engineer, or are in a highly specialized line of businesses—be doubly careful when you talk to outsiders to express yourself in *plain terms*, and to fill in necessary details.

Put your ideas into language plain enough for any boy to understand.

Chapter Nine

How to Interest Your Audience

What would you say are the three most interesting subjects in the world? They are: *sex, property,* and *religion*. By the first we can create life, by the second we maintain it, and by the third we hope to continue it in the world to come.

But it is *our* sex, *our* property, and *our* religion that interests us. Our interests swarm around our own egos.

When a British newspaper baron was asked what interests people, he answered with one word: "themselves." Do you want to know what kind of person you are? Ah, now we are on an interesting topic. We are talking about *you*.

Remember that people spend most of their time, when they are not concerned with the problems of business, thinking about and justifying and glorifying themselves. The average man will be more wrought up over a dull razor than over a revolution in South America. His own toothache will distress him more than an earthquake in Asia destroying half-a-million lives. He would rather listen to you say some nice thing about him than hear you discuss the ten greatest men in history.

A successful magazine editor once told me the secret of capturing people's attention: "People are selfish," he said. "They are interested chiefly in themselves. They are not very much concerned about whether the government should own the railroads; but they do want to know how to get ahead, how to draw more salary, how to keep healthy, how to take care of their teeth, how to take baths, how to keep cool in the summer, how to get a job, how to handle employees, how to buy homes, how to remember, how to avoid grammatical errors, and so one. People are always interested in human stories, so I have some rich man tell how he made a million in real estate. I get prominent bankers and presidents of various corporations to tell their stories of how they battled their way up to power and wealth."

This editor has attracted millions of readers by appealing to their selfish interests.

But interest is also *contagious*. Your hearers are almost sure to catch it if you have a bad case of it yourself. A short time ago I heard a speaker warn his audience that if the present methods of catching rockfish in Chesapeake Bay were continued the species would become extinct. And in a very few years! He *felt* his subject. It was important. He was in real earnest about it. When he finished all of us probably would have been willing to sign a petition to protect the rockfish by law.

Always remember, your audience will feel interested in your topic to the degree that you are sincerely interested in it yourself.

Chapter Ten

Improving Your Language

The world judges us by four things: by what we do, by how we look, by what we say, and by how we say it.

Many people blunder through life with no conscious effort to enrich their stock of words, to master their shades of meaning, and to speak with precision. Many people habitually use the overworked and exhausted phrases of the office and street. Small wonder that their way of speaking lacks distinction and individuality.

But how are we to become intimate with words, to speak them with beauty and accuracy? Fortunately, there is no mystery about the means to be employed. *Books!* There is the secret. He who would enlarge his stock of words must drink deeply of good literature.

Lincoln wrote to a young man eager to become a successful lawyer: "It is only to get the books, and read and study them carefully . . . Work, work, work is the main thing."

What books? Begin with Arnold Bennett's *How to Live on Twenty-Four Hours a Day*. This book is as stimulating as a cold bath. It tells you a lot about that most interesting of all subjects—yourself. It reveals how much time you are wasting each day, how to stop the wastage, and how to use what you salvage.

To learn about greatness, make Ralph Waldo Emerson your daily companion. Command him first to give you his famous essay on "Self-Reliance." Read it again and again. Dedicate yourself to Emerson's essays and you will encounter some of the highest thoughts and finest uses of words in the English language.

Finally, don't use shopworn, threadbare words and expressions. Be exact in your meaning. Avoid trite comparisons such as "cool as a cucumber" or "high as a kite." Strive for freshness. Create expressions of your own. Have the courage to be distinctive.

CHAPTER ELEVEN

How to Get Action

I f you could have the power of any talent that you now possess doubled and tripled, which one would you select? Wouldn't you likely designate your ability to influence others, to get action? That would mean additional power, additional profit, and additional pleasure.

Must this art—so essential to our success in life—remain forever a hit-and-miss affair? Must we blunder along depending upon our instinct, upon rule-of-thumb methods only? Or is there a more intelligent way to achieve it?

There is, and we shall discuss it at once—a method based on the rules of common sense, on the rules of human nature, a method that I have frequently, and successfully, used myself.

The first step in this method is to gain *interested attention*. Unless you do that people will not listen closely to what you say. We've already touched on some of the ways to do this: Talk to people about topics of vital interest—usually themselves. Be deeply in earnest about what you say. Be clear, plainspoken, and definite as to what you mean.

The second step is to gain the *confidence* of your hearers. Unless you do that, they will have no faith in what you say. And here is where many speakers fall down. Here is where many advertisements fail, where many business letters, many employees, many business enterprises go nowhere. Here is where many individuals fail to make themselves effective within the human environment.

The prime way to win confidence is to *deserve it.* I have noticed time without number that facile and witty speakers—if those are their chief qualities—are not nearly as effective as those who are less brilliant but more sincere. There is no use trying to pretend a sympathy or sincerity that one does not feel. It won't work. It must be genuine.

The second way to gain the confidence of the audience is to speak discretely out of your own experience. This helps immensely. If you give opinions, people may question them. If you relate hearsay or repeat what you have read, it may have a second-hand flavor. But what *you yourself have lived through*, that has a genuine ring of truth and veracity. And people like it. They believe it.

Once you have won people's confidence, consider what people are looking for—from you and from the world around them. One of the strongest of human motives is *the desire for gain*. And even stronger than the money motive is the desire for *self-protection*. All health appeals are based on that. To make an appeal to someone's sense of self-protection, make it personal. Don't, for example, quote statistics to show that cancer is on the rise. No. Tie it right down to the people who are listening to you, for example: "There are thirty people in this room. If all of you live to be forty-five, three of you, according to the law of medical averages, will die of cancer."

As strong as the desire for money—and for many even stronger—is the wish to be well regarded, to be admired. In other words, pride. Ask yourself why you bought this book. Were you influenced, to some extent, by the wish to make a better impression? Did you covet the flow of inward satisfaction that comes from making a commendable talk? Won't you feel a very pardonable pride in the power, leadership, and distinction that naturally flow to the good public speaker?

There is another powerful group of motives that influence us mightily. We shall call them religious motives. I mean religious not in the sense of orthodox worship or the tenets of any particular creed or sect. I mean rather that broad group of beautiful and eternal truths that Christ taught: justice and forgiveness and mercy, serving others and loving our neighbors as ourselves.

No man likes to admit, even to himself, that he is not good and kind and magnanimous. So we love to be appealed to on these grounds. It implies a certain nobleness of soul. We take pride in that.

To summarize all we have been discussing, here are the ways that you as a speaker can get people on your side and move them to action:

FIRST
Get interested attention.

SECOND
Win confidence by deserving it, not only by your sincerity but also by being qualified to speak on your subject, by telling us the things that experience has taught you.

THIRD
State your facts clearly and educate your audience regarding the merits of your proposal or cause.

FOURTH
Appeal to the motives that make us act: the desire for gain, self-protection, pride, pleasures, sentiments, affec-

tions, and religious ideals, such as justice, mercy, forgiveness, and love.

These methods, if used wisely, will not only help the speaker in public, but also in private. They will help him in the writing of sales letters, in constructing advertisements, in managing business interviews—and in making an impact in life.

About the Authors

Born in northwestern Missouri in 1888, Dale Carnegie was one of the pioneers of motivational and self-help philosophy. World famous for his 1936 classic, *How to Win Friends and Influence People*, Carnegie began his career as a writer and teacher in 1912 when he offered courses on public speaking at a YMCA in New York City. Carnegie was one of the first business minds of the twentieth century to grasp the importance of being able to communicate ideas and concepts clearly to colleagues, coworkers, clients, and customers. His pioneering book, *Public Speaking: A Practical Course for Business Men*, from which this volume is abridged, first appeared in 1926. It is regarded as the seminal work on how to speak with power and skill. Carnegie died in New York City in 1955.

Mitch Horowitz, who abridged and introduced this volume, is the PEN Award-winning author of books including *Occult America* and *The Miracle Club: How Thoughts Become Reality*. *The Washington Post* says Mitch "treats esoteric ideas and movements with an even-handed intellectual studiousness that is too often lost in today's raised-voice discussions." Follow him @MitchHorowitz.